OLYMPIC EXPERT

Paul Mason

W

FRANKLIN WATTS

LONDON • SYDNEY

Franklin Watts

First published in Great Britain in 2016 by The Watts Publishing Group

Series Editor: Julia Bird

Series Designer: D.R.Ink

Picture credits: Action Plus/Alamy: 27t. Action Plus/Topfoto: 14. AFP/Getty Images: 4t, 23t. AP/PAI: 12. Fabrizio Bensch/AFP/Getty Images: 5b. Jefferson Bernardes/Shutterstock: 29. Bettmann/Corbis: 7t, 19b. Shaunn Botterill/Getty Images: 15b. Simon Bruty/Sports Illustrated/Getty Images: 18t. Thomas Coex/AFP/Getty Images: 13. Fabrice Coffrini/AFP/Getty Images: 5t. Piero Cruciatti/Dreamstime: front cover cl. Bob Daemmrich/Alamy: 27b. Darrensharvey/Dreamstime: 22. Stu Forster/Getty Images: 20r. Gamma-Rapho/Getty Images: 17b. Geraldkf/Dreamstime: 17t. Paul Gilham/Getty Images: 11t. Glypothek Munich/wikimedia commons: 18. Mitch Gunn/Shutterstock: 2, 6. Scott Heavey/Getty Images: 8. Harry How/Getty Images: 15t. Bob Jones/Rex Shutterstock: front cover tl. Kenshi991/Shutterstock: 31b. Thomas Kienzle/AP/PAI: front cover b, 16t. Paul Kitagaki Jr./Getty Images: 9. David E Klutho/Getty Images: 7b. Korean Olympic Committee: 3, 25b. Alex Livesey/Getty Images: 24. Manny Millan/Sports Ilustrated/Getty Images: 20l, 30. Popperfoto/Getty Images: 21. Mike Powell/Getty Images: 11b. Celso Pupo/Shutterstock: 28. Michael Reagan/Getty Images: 25t. Rkaphotography/Dreamstime: 10, 26. Christopher Simon/AFP/Getty Images: 16b, 31t. Split Seconds/Alamy: front cover cr, 7c. Ullsteinbild/Getty Images: 23b. Phil Walter/Getty Images: front cover tr. wikimedia commons: 4b.

Dewey number: 790

HB ISBN 978 1 4451 4821 2

Library ebook ISBN 978 1 4451 4823 6

Printed in China

Franklin Watts, an imprint of

Hachette Children's Group

Part of The Watts Publishing Group
Carmelite House
50 Victoria Embankment
London EC4Y 0DZ

An Hachette UK Company

www.hachette.co.uk

www.franklinwatts.co.uk

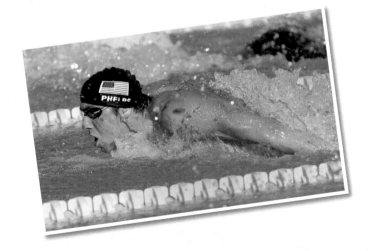

CONTENTS

THE GREATEST SHOW ON EARTH

The opening ceremony to the 2012 Olympics celebrated UK life and culture.

"Faster, higher, stronger."

– the Olympic motto.

The Olympic Games are the world's biggest show. Over half of the people on Earth – 3.6 billion of them – watched the 2012 Olympics in London. That's the same as the entire population of the world in 1970! In Britain alone, the opening ceremony was seen by 27 million people.

A bit of history

The Olympics were first held in Olympia in Greece in 776 BCE – but things were a bit different back then. There were running events like today's, but also chariot racing. And the boxing, wrestling and *pankration* (a kind of MMA) were so violent that competitors sometimes died! Women were not allowed to take part, or even to spectate. In most events, the competitors appeared naked just to be sure none were female. The ancient Olympics stopped in 394 CE.

Pankration was a brutal combination of boxing and wrestling.

CRAZY GAMES

The craziest Olympics EVER were the Paris 1900 Games. Sports included an underwater swimming race (which spectators found hard to enjoy); various ballooning contests; rope climbing; and croquet!

The modern Olympics

Imagine turning on the TV to watch the Olympic contest for landing a hot air balloon, firefighting or pigeon-racing. Those are just a few of the crazy events from the early days of the modern Olympics.

The modern Olympics started out in the 1890s. A French aristocrat called Baron Pierre de Coubertin had the idea. The Games were to be held in a different country every four years. The first modern Olympics were held in 1896, in Athens, Greece. Only 241 athletes turned

TECHNICALLY SPEAKING...

Olympic rewards

The top three competitors in an Olympic event get gold, silver and bronze medals. Between 1904 and 1912, the medals were made of real gold. This was a big improvement on 1900, when some top finishers were given paintings as prizes.

The 5000m medal-winners at the 2008 Olympics proudly display their medals.

up! These days, the Games get more popular each time they are held (possibly because pigeon-racing has been replaced by more sporty activities). The 2012 Olympics were the biggest ever, with more than 10,000 athletes representing over 200 different places.

China's team parade at the opening ceremony of the 2012 Olympics.

AQUATIC SPORTS

Michael Phelps swimming butterfly – one of the few events he didn't win at the 2012 Olympics.

Back at the Athens Olympics of 1896, competitors in some swimming events were taken out to sea in boats and told to swim back to shore! Aquatic sports have changed a bit since then....

AMAZING OLYMPIANS

NAME: Michael Phelps

COUNTRY: USA

At the 2008 Olympics in Beijing, swimmer Michael Phelps set a record by winning eight gold medals at a single Games. Then in 2012, he became the most successful Olympian ever. By the end of the London Games, he had won a career total of 22 medals – 18 of them gold!

TECHNICALLY SPEAKING...

In theory, swimmers can use any stroke in a freestyle race. In reality, everyone swims front crawl because it is the fastest stroke.

Swimming

Today, the only aquatic event not held in a pool is the 'marathon' – which is actually 10km, not 42km like a running marathon. The marathon swim is held outdoors.

In the pool there are four strokes: backstroke, breaststroke, butterfly and front crawl. Most races are for individuals, but there are also relays for teams of swimmers. The fastest 16 from the heats go through to the semi-finals. The fastest eight from the semi-finals get a place in the final. The quicker swimmers race in the middle lanes, the slower ones in the outer lanes.

WATCH OUT FOR:

The men's 4x100m freestyle relay. The USA have won this eight times, including every year from 1964 to 1996. In 2012, though, France grabbed the gold – and the Americans weren't happy!

CRAZY GAMES

The 1956 Olympic water polo final was between Hungary and the USSR. Weeks before, the USSR had invaded Hungary. The match quickly became violent. When Prokopov of the USSR punched Hungary's Ervin Zador (above), fans became so angry that the spectator area had to be cleared. Hungary won 4–0.

Water polo

Water polo is a swimming version of football, with seven players per team. Teams have to shoot within 30 seconds of getting the ball, which makes for plenty of action.

Diving

Dives are from either the 10m platform or the 3m springboard. There are contests for individuals and synchronised diving (where pairs try to time their movements exactly together). The divers are scored based on how well they did the dive and how difficult it was.

Synchronised swimming

At the Olympics, synchronised swimming is women-only, although it has been suggested that men may soon take part. 'Synchro' is a kind of dancing in water; there are contests for pairs and teams.

China's women's synchronised divers show off their gold medal-winning routine in 2012.

The Australian synchronised swimming team at the 2012 Olympics.

COMBAT SPORTS

The Olympic Games have a long tradition of fighting. The ancient Olympics featured lots of warlike events, and today there are four different combat sports on the Olympic programme.

Boxing

Boxing has appeared at every Olympics since 1904 – except the 1912 Olympics in Stockholm. Boxing missed out in 1912 because back then, it was illegal in Sweden.

Men's fights take place over three 3-minute rounds. Women, who started boxing at the Games in 2012, fight four 2-minute rounds. Boxers score a point by punching the head or body of their opponent. The punch has to land above the belt, and they must hit with the knuckles of their glove.

Judo

Judo is popular all round the world, and people from all six inhabited continents have won Olympic judo medals. Most, though, have come from Asia. After the 2012 Olympics, Japan had won 36 golds – three times as many as the next-highest (France, with 12).

Nicola Adams celebrates her historic Olympic boxing win.

AMAZING OLYMPIANS

NAME: Nicola Adams

COUNTRY: Great Britain

On 9 August 2012, in eight thrilling minutes of boxing, Adams beat the Chinese world champion boxer Ren Cancan by 16 points to 7 – and became the first EVER women's Olympic boxing champion.

In Greco-Roman wrestling, only holds above the waist are allowed. This makes throws the main form of attack.

Wrestling

There are two styles of wrestling at the Olympics: Greco-Roman, which is only for men, and freestyle, which has men's and women's competitions. The aim is to win by forcing your opponent's shoulders to the ground for two seconds, or to get points by making a throw or 'take down'.

Taekwondo

The first Olympic medals for taekwondo were awarded at the 2000 Olympics in Sydney, and the sport is now very popular. It is fast-moving and spectacular, with punches and high kicks. The fights last for three 2-minute rounds, but if the scores are equal at the end, there is a fourth round. This is known as 'sudden death'. The first fighter to score wins.

CRAZY GAMES

One of the biggest Olympic sulks ever was by South Korea's Byun Jong-il in 1988. After losing a boxing match, he refused to leave the ring. Byun sat there for 67 minutes – and only finally left when the stadium was empty and the officials turned out the lights.

CYCLING

There has been cycling at every Olympics since the Athens Olympics of 1896, where French cyclist Paul Masson won three of the six events. Today, there are 18 cycling events. They are split between four types of racing: track, road, BMX and mountain bike.

Road racing

The Olympic road race is held between national teams. Usually one rider is the leader. The others are there to shield the leader from the wind, chase attacks by rivals, and fetch drinks and food from the team car that follows behind. The men's road race is about 250km long. The women's race is about 150km.

There is also a time-trial competition, in which riders set off one by one, striving to cover the course in the fastest possible time.

BMX

The exciting BMX competition features jumps, bumps and crashes. The riders race out of a start gate, down a ramp, and around a swooping bike obstacle course. A fast start is crucial: it is tricky to overtake in BMX, and the leading rider gets a clear run at the jumps, turns and other obstacles.

AMAZING OLYMPIANS

NAME: Sir Bradley Wiggins
COUNTRY: Great Britain

After winning three Olympic gold medals at the 2004 and 2008 Olympics, Wiggins left track cycling for road racing. He won time-trial gold at the 2012 Games (weeks after winning the gruelling road race, the Tour de France). In 2014, 'Wiggo' announced that he was aiming to return to track competition at the 2016 Olympics.

Cheered on by his home crowd, Wiggo rides for gold at the 2012 Olympics.

CRAZY GAMES

At the 1964 Tokyo Olympics, two riders in the individual sprint event stood motionless, balancing on the pedals of their bikes, for nearly TWENTY-TWO minutes. Each was waiting for the other to go first.

Mountain biking

Cross-country mountain bike courses can be no more than 15 per cent flat – the rest has to be uphill or downhill! Races are about 40km in total, with men's races longer than women's. Olympic courses are usually about 5km long, so the riders go round them many times.

Track cycling

Track riders race around an indoor circuit with steep banking. At its steepest the track slopes inward at 42° – it's hard to even stand up on! Riding at the top of the banking, near the barriers, lets riders accelerate 'downhill' onto the straight. They reach speeds of over 100 kph – on bikes that only have one gear and no brakes!

Most mountain-bikers ride 'hardtail' bikes, with suspension only at the front.

AMAZING OLYMPIANS

NAME: Anna Meares

COUNTRY: Australia

Meares won the 500m time-trial gold on the cycling track at the 2004 Olympics, but had a terrible crash months before the 2008 Games. Despite suffering a broken neck vertebra she managed to qualify for the Games, and won silver behind Britain's Victoria Pendleton in the women's sprint. In 2012, she went one better and beat Pendleton to the gold medal.

The steep banking of the London Olympic Velodrome.

GYMNASTICS

Nadia Comaneci performs a balanced jump at the 1976 Olympics.

Gymnastics has been part of the modern Olympics since 1896. At first, events such as rope climbing and club swinging were included, and only men took part. Today there are three main gymnastics competitions: artistic, rhythmic and trampoline.

Artistic gymnastics

In the 1900s, many people (including lots of armies) did gymnastic exercises for fitness. Artistic gymnastics was given its name to show it was more flowing than these military-style exercises. At first gymnastics was only for men, but by 1952 women also had a full programme.

Today, there are eight events for men and six for women. There is one for each piece of apparatus, plus an individual all-round contest and a team contest.

London 2012

Team Japan perform their three ribbons and two hoops routine during the final of the rhythmic gymnastics event at the 2012 Olympics.

Rhythmic gymnastics

Rhythmic gymnastics is a floor-based competition, which first became part of the Olympics in 1984. Gymnasts use apparatus such as balls, hoops and ribbons, and perform a routine set to music. There are individual and team contests, and the competition is for women only.

Trampoline

Trampolining became part of the Olympic gymnastics programme in 2000. In the crowd watching was the 86-year-old inventor of the trampoline, George Nissen. He originally created the trampoline as a way to practise other sports, but it was so much fun that it soon became popular on its own. At the Olympics, trampolinists perform flips and twists while bouncing up to 10m high.

TECHNICALLY SPEAKING...

Scoring in artistic gymnastics has changed since the days of Nadia Comaneci. Now, gymnasts start with an 'execution score' of 10, which the judges reduce according to how many mistakes are made. This score is added to a 'difficulty score' that is based on the technical difficulty of their performance.

BOAT SPORTS

The organisers originally planned to include rowing and sailing competitions at the 1896 Olympics – but the weather was stormy and there were too few sailing boats, so the races never happened! Competitors today have spent years training in all sorts of conditions.

AMAZING OLYMPIANS

NAME: Ben Ainslie

COUNTRY: Great Britain

Ainslie has an amazing record in Olympic sailing competitions. He won gold medals at the 2000, 2004, 2008 and 2012 Olympics. This makes him the most successful sailor in Olympic history.

Sailing

There are six sailing events for men, and four for women. All are for different types of sailboat, except for the men's and women's windsurfing races. The racers follow a course that is laid out so that they have to sail into, away from and across the wind. This tests all their sailing skills.

Ben Ainslie squeezes every knot of speed from his dinghy at the 2012 Olympics.

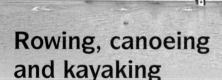

Rowing, canoeing and kayaking

Rowing events take place on a flat, straight course of 2km. There are two basic types of rowing. The first is when each rower has one oar, and the oars stick out on alternate sides of the boat. The second is sculling, when the rowers use two oars, one in each hand.

Sprint canoeing and kayaking also take place on the rowing course. They cover shorter distances, between 200m and 1km.

It's not only the rowers who work hard – look at the coaches cycling alongside!

CRAZY GAMES

At the 1928 Amsterdam Olympics, Australia's Henry Pearce stopped rowing in his quarter-final race so that he did not run over a passing family of ducks! He still won the quarter-final, plus gold in the final.

Whitewater

In whitewater events, canoeists and kayakers steer their boats down a raging stream of water. There are steep drops, rocks to avoid and rapid changes of direction. Contestants pass through a series of gates – sometimes even through a gate heading upstream. The fastest wins, but there are time penalties if you touch a gate.

TECHNICALLY SPEAKING...

In Olympic sailing contests, the scores are decided using the results of a series of races. Racers get one point for a win, two for second and so on. At the end, the ten best racers take part in the 'medal race', in which the points are doubled.

Michal Martikán of Slovakia has won canoeing medals at every Olympic Games between 1996 and 2012.

TRACK ATHLETICS

The ancient Olympics featured a race called *stadion*, a sprint of about 200m. There were also longer races, and even one where the athletes wore armour. Running has been part of the Games ever since.

AMAZING OLYMPIANS

NAME: Usain Bolt

COUNTRY: Jamaica

'The Lightning Bolt' is the best Olympic sprinter ever. In 2008 he won gold in the 100m, 200m and 4x100m relay – all in world record times. Then at London 2012 he won the same three events.

WATCH OUT FOR:

The men's 100m final is probably the most-watched event of the entire Olympics. In 2012, an estimated 20 million people watched Usain Bolt's winning run.

Sprints

Sprint races are held over 100m, 200m and 400m, plus a 4x100m and 4x400m relay. These are favourites with the crowd. The competition is fierce; the winner of the 100m can say that he or she was the fastest runner at the Olympics.

As well as flat sprints, there are sprint hurdles races. In the short races, men run 110m and women 100m. There are also 400m hurdles races.

In the 110m hurdles, the runners only have time for three strides between hurdles.

The marathon at the London 1908 Olympics was a disaster! Canada's Tom Longboat collapsed while in the lead. Charles Hefferon of South Africa took over, but then fell ill. Italy's Dorando Pietri hit the front – but was so tired he collapsed five times in the last 200 metres, was carried over the finish line, and got disqualified. Johnny Hayes of the USA finally won – and had to be carried around his victory lap on a table!

Leading marathon runners pass the London Eye during the 2012 Olympics.

AMAZING OLYMPIANS

NAME: Cathy Freeman

COUNTRY: Australia

Not only an Australian, Freeman is an Aboriginal Australian. In the 2000 Sydney Olympics 400m final, she represented both communities. Freeman won in 49.11 seconds – making her only the second-ever Aboriginal-Australian gold medallist.

Middle distance

Middle distance races range from 800m to 1500m; 3000m races are also sometimes included in this category. At the Olympics the only 3000m is the steeplechase. In this, the runners leap over barriers, including a tricky water jump.

Long distance

The longest running race is the marathon, which covers 42.195km. The marathon distance is based on a legendary run in ancient Greece in 490 BCE. A soldier called Pheidippides ran from the Battle of Marathon to Athens with news of an Athenian victory. Pheidippides then collapsed and died! The marathon takes place on roads, so the host city always plots a course that shows off the best sights. Walking races of 20km and 50km are also held on roads. On track, the long-distance races are the 5000m and 10,000m.

FIELD ATHLETICS

Field athletics events have been part of the Olympics since ancient times. Discus-throwing, javelin and long jump were all in the original Games. Today there are eight different field sports at the Olympics.

Discus, hammer, javelin and shot put

These are all throwing events, which suit big, extremely strong athletes. Javelin throwers use a run-up; the others all throw from inside a small circle. Most use a spinning technique to add maximum distance to their throws. They need excellent balance – if the thrower steps out of the front of the circle, the throw will not count.

AMAZING OLYMPIANS

NAME: Jan Železný

COUNTRY: Czech Republic

The best Olympic javelin thrower ever, Železný holds the world record with a throw of 98.48m. At the 1988 Olympics Železný led the whole event – until he was beaten by Tapio Korjus of Finland with the very LAST throw. It did not happen again: Železny won in 1992, 1996 and 2000.

This bronze statue shows an Ancient Olympic discus-thrower.

Yelena Isinbayeva of Russia, winner of pole vault gold at the 2004 and 2008 Olympics.

CRAZY GAMES

Between 1900 and 1920, one of the hottest tickets at the Olympics was the tug-of-war. To win, you had to pull the other team forward 1.83m. In 1908, the gold was won by the team from the London police force.

CRAZY GAMES

At the 1968 Olympics in Mexico City, Bob Beamon of the USA broke the long jump world record with a jump of 8.90m. It was so far that the official measuring device wasn't long enough to record the distance!

High jump and pole vault

In high jump, athletes use only their own speed and technique to leap over the bar. Pole vaulters use a long, bendy pole to boost them high into the air. In both events, failing to get over the bar three times in a row (including at different heights) means you leave the competition.

Long jump and triple jump

There are also contests for who can jump the furthest. In the early 1900s, there were long jump and triple jump competitions from a standing start, but today athletes use a run-up. Long jump is a single jump. Triple jump is a sequence of hop (landing on the same foot as you took off from); step (land on the other foot); and jump (land both feet together).

MULTI-SPORT EVENTS

Heptathletes need the sprint speed and technique of a hurdler...

...the skills of a high jumper – and the strength of a javelin thrower!

Multi-sport events are a tough challenge. It is not enough to be world class at one sport. In the largest multi-sport event – decathlon – you have to be good at ten!

Decathlon and heptathlon

At the Olympics, decathlon is for men and heptathlon for women. Both competitions are made up of a mixture of track and field events. The men take part in ten events, the women seven. The athletes score points in each event. The closer they get to the world record, the more points they score. The winner is the one with most points when all events are finished.

Modern pentathlon

Pentathlon is made up of five events. The first three are fencing, swimming and show-jumping. After these, there is a combined running and shooting race. The athletes must hit a target five times (or keep shooting for 50 seconds), then run 800m. They do this four times, making 3200m and 20 hits (or 3 minutes 20 seconds of shooting) in total.

CRAZY GAMES

Tunisia's modern pentathlon team did not cover themselves in glory at the 1960 Olympics. In the swimming, one of them nearly drowned. All three fell off their horses in the show-jumping. They were asked to leave the shooting contest after almost shooting one of the judges. And only one could fence – so he kept his mask on the whole time and pretended to be the others, as well as himself!

AMAZING OLYMPIANS

NAME: Alistair and Jonathan Brownlee

COUNTRY: Great Britain

The Brownlee brothers are a triathlon double act: if one does not win, the other often does. In 2012 it was Alistair who was ahead, winning Olympic gold. Jonathan got bronze, making them the first brothers to be on the same Olympic podium since 1908.

Seen here in the 2012 triathlon, the Brownlees are leaving the transition area, where the bikes are left, and starting the running leg.

Triathlon

Triathlon was invented in the 1970s, as a way for track athletes to make their training interesting. It soon became a separate sport; the first Olympic triathlon was held in 2000. The triathlon is usually one of the first events at the Olympics. The athletes swim 1500m, cycle 40km and run 10km. The run is the crucial part of the triathlon: saving enough energy for this leg is as important as doing well in the earlier sports.

TEAM SPORTS

The most popular team sport at the Olympics is probably football. During the 2012 Olympics, it was definitely the sport mentioned most often on Twitter – five million times!

WATCH OUT FOR:

Rugby sevens – new to the 2016 Olympics, this fast-paced sport is exciting to watch, and sometimes produces surprise winners.

Football

There is a rumour that football was played at the first modern Olympics, in 1896 – but there is no official record of it. Men's football has *definitely* been part of the Games since 1900. The only Olympics since then without a football competition was Los Angeles in 1932, where it was replaced by American football. Women's football first appeared at the Olympics in 1996.

Mexico (in red) take on Gabon at the 2012 Olympics

Shot-blocking is a crucial volleyball skill.

Volleyball

There are two kinds of volleyball at the Olympics. In the standard game, two teams of six players try to hit the ball across the net and onto the ground on the other side. The other team tries to stop the ball hitting the ground. Teams can only touch the ball three times before sending it back over the net. Beach volleyball is a version of the same game for two players per team, played on a sandy court.

Hockey

In hockey, two teams of 11 players use sticks to pass and shoot a small, hard ball. The aim is to score goals, and the team with most goals wins. New timings were introduced for the 2016 Olympics (see page 28–29), with each game lasting four 15-minute quarters.

Rugby

At the Olympics, teams play a version of rugby called 'sevens'. It is fast-moving and exciting, and plenty of tries are scored. Each game takes just 14 minutes, so the crowd gets to see several games within a short time.

India's captain Balbir Singh on the winner's rostrum at the 1956 Olympics.

AMAZING OLYMPIANS

NAME: India men's hockey team

COUNTRY: India

India's men's hockey team won every Olympic gold between 1924 and 1956. That makes 35 years as Olympic champions!* In 1960, the title was won by their bitter rivals, Pakistan, but India still won again in 1964 and 1980.

(*32 years from 1924 to 1956, plus three years to the next Olympics.)

MINORITY SPORT REPORT

At least 141 medals will be handed out at the 2016 Olympics – for athletics alone! Sports like athletics, swimming and cycling, where lots of medals are won, get most attention. But there are many other sports to watch at the Olympics.

Equestrian sports

There are three equestrian competitions. In dressage, the riders and horses perform a difficult routine of carefully controlled movements. In show-jumping, the horses have to complete a course of 8–12 jumps without any mistakes, in the fastest time possible. Eventing is a combination of dressage, jumping and timed cross-country riding.

CRAZY GAMES

The 1900 Olympics featured two events that have since disappeared: the long jump and high jump... for horses.

Because of Australia's tough quarantine rules, all the equestrian events at the 1956 Olympics were actually held in Sweden – 15,600 km away.

Knocking bars from a jump is known as a 'fault' and affects your result.

CRAZY GAMES

The only time animals have intentionally been harmed during the Games was at the Paris Olympics in 1900. The events included pigeon shooting – at live pigeons, rather than the clay discs that are used today.

Tennis, badminton and table tennis

In table tennis, tennis and badminton, there are men's and women's contests for single players and 'doubles', or two players. In tennis and badminton there is also a mixed doubles event, with teams of one man and one woman.

Archery and shooting

In archery, there are individual and team events. The archers shoot at a target that is 70m away. Even hitting it would be tricky for most people! The shooting competitions are more varied. Depending on the event, the target could be anything from 10m to 50m away. The guns used in shooting contests include air pistols, rifles and shotguns. The shooters usually stand up to shoot, but there are also 'prone' competitions, where they lie down.

Golf

Before 2016, every Olympic golf medallist came from North America. Margaret Abbott and Charles Sands of the USA won in 1900, and George Lyon of Canada won in 1904. After that, golf disappeared from the list of Olympic sports… until finally, 112 years later, it reappeared for the 2016 Games.

AMAZING OLYMPIANS

Between 1984 and 2012, archers from South Korea have won an amazing 14 out of 15 possible gold medals in women's competitions.

Choi Hyeon-Ju of South Korea lines up the target in the women's team event at the 2012 Olympics.

THE PARALYMPICS

"Spirit in motion."

– the Paralympic motto.

Almost since the Olympic Games began, people with disabilities have been taking part. In 1904, the gymnast George Eyser won three gold medals in a day – despite having an artificial leg. But from 1960, disabled athletes have had a separate Games of their own.

AMAZING OLYMPIANS

NAME: David Weir

COUNTRY: UK

Born unable to use his legs, Weir (below) is one of the UK's most successful wheelchair racers of all time. At the 2008 and 2012 Paralympics, he won a total of six gold medals. Weir's wins were at distances ranging from 800m to marathon.

Paralympics today

Today, over 4,000 athletes come to the Paralympics, and there are 20 different sports to take part in. Athletics, swimming and cycling are all popular, but the Games include specialist sports too. Look out for wheelchair basketball, fencing, rugby and *boccia,* a similar game to bowls and *pétanque.*

Wheelchair racing legend David Weir leads in the 2012 Paralympics T54 marathon.

Natalie du Toit powers through the water in a 200m heat in 2008.

WATCH OUT FOR:
GOALBALL!

Goalball is a bit like a cross between 5-a-side football and bowling, played by blind and visually impaired athletes. The ball contains bells, so that players can work out where it is. Teams of three try to score by rolling the ball into the opposition's goal.

All goalball players wear blindfolds to make the game fair.

Paralympic standouts

Just to get to the Paralympics you have to be a great athlete. But there are a few competitors whose amazing abilities make them stand out:

- Trischa Zorn of the USA has won more medals than any other Paralympian. Between 1980 and 2004 she took part in blind swimming competitions. When she retired from racing in 2004, Zorn had 55 medals – 41 of them gold.

- Canadian Chantal Petitclerc won 14 golds in women's wheelchair racing. Amazingly, at the 2004 Paralympics she won the 100m, 200m, 400m, 800m and 1500m races. Then she did it again in 2008.

- South African Natalie du Toit (above) swam in the 2008 Olympics and Paralympics – making her one of the few people to take part in both Games in the same year.

RIO 2016

"Rio will deliver an unforgettable Games."

– Brazil's former president Lula

Welcome to Rio de Janeiro, Brazil: site of the 2016 Olympics. These Games are the first to have been held in South America. Rio is a spectacular choice, with the blue Atlantic Ocean on the city's doorstep and steep-sided hills all around.

The Olympic Games in 2016 last 17 days, and over 10,000 athletes from 205 different places take part. There are 42 sports and 306 medal events. The action is spread between four main areas:

Barra

This neighbourhood of Rio is famous for its beaches, lakes and parks. It is the biggest location for the Games, with over half the events being held here. The main Olympic Park hosts swimming, gymnastics, tennis, and combat sports such as wrestling and judo.

WATCH OUT FOR:

Golf, which is back in the Olympics for the first time since 1904, and rugby, which has not appeared at the Games since 1924.

Copacabana

Copacabana is probably the most famous beach in Brazil, and it's home to one of Brazil's favourite sports: beach volleyball. Sailing, rowing, triathlon and open-water swimming are all happening nearby, in the calmer waters north of Fort Copacabana.

Deodoro

The second-biggest Olympic venue, Deodoro is home to traditional and modern sports. Equestrian events happen here, as do shooting and modern pentathlon. Nearby, the X-Park has facilities for mountain biking, BMX, and whitewater canoeing and kayaking.

Maracanã

The famous football stadium at Maracanã holds almost 80,000 spectators, and every seat is already booked for the opening and closing ceremonies of the Olympics. The same is true of Brazil's matches in the Olympic football competition. Maracanã also hosts the athletics competitions, archery, volleyball and water polo.

CRAZY GAMES

The Olympic Stadium at Maracanã once contained the world's biggest football crowd. In 1950, 173,850 people watched Brazil take on Uruguay – and lose!

Olympic brain-ache: test yourself

1 When did the gold medals in the Olympics stop being made of real gold?

  a After World War II, when there was a global shortage
  b 1912, (when they became too expensive)
  c They are still made of solid gold

2 In sailing, the winner is the person with...?

  a The fewest points
  b The most points
  c The sailor who crosses the line first in the last race

3 How many events are there in modern pentathlon?

  a One – modern pentathlon
  b Five – obviously, because pente is Greek for 'five'
  c It's a trick question – four

4 Olympic events are not always held in the host city. What is the furthest away an Olympic event has ever been held?

  a 200km, the distance between London 2012 and the sailing events held at Weymouth, Dorset
  b 3,800km, the distance between Rio 2016 and the Olympic football stadium in Manaus, Amazonia
  c 15,600km, the distance between Melbourne 1956 and the equestrian centre in Stockholm, Sweden

5 Which of these events were part of the ancient Olympics?

  a Wrestling, boxing, javelin and discus
  b 200m and marathon
  c All of the above

Answers
1 b; 2 a; 3 c (it is a trick question: the last two sports – running and shooting – are combined in one event); 4 c (though the other distances are also quite far!); 5 a (a race of nearly 200m called stadion was in the ancient Games, but the marathon was not).

Olympic sports in full

There are 28 different categories of Olympic sport, but some contain very different activities. Each activity may have lots of events. For example, there are 10 different medals available in track cycling, which is just one of the four cycling activities.

Here is a full list of the Olympic sports. You can find out more about each of them on the International Olympic Committee website, at www.olympic.org. There are lots of details of the 2016 Games at Rio de Janeiro at www.rio2016.com.

Aquatics

- Diving
- Swimming
- Synchronised swimming
- Water polo

Archery

Athletics

Badminton

Basketball

Boxing

Canoe

- Slalom
- Sprint

Cycling

- BMX
- Road
- Track
- Mountain bike

Equestrian

- Dressage
- Eventing
- Jumping

Fencing

Football

Golf

Gymnastics

- Artistic
- Rhythmic
- Trampoline

Handball

Hockey

Judo

Modern pentathlon

Rowing

Rugby

Sailing

Shooting

Table tennis

Taekwondo

Tennis

Triathlon

Volleyball

- Beach volleyball
- Volleyball

Weightlifting

Wrestling

- Freestyle
- Greco-Roman

Glossary

apparatus piece of equipment used in gymnastics

bar horizontal pole that high jumpers and long jumpers try to get over without knocking it down

demonstration sport sport included to test and increase its popularity

doubles with two players per side

equestrian to do with horses

fixed wheel bike on which the back wheel and pedals always turn together, so that all the time the bike is moving the rider has to keep pedalling

gates in whitewater sports, pairs of poles hanging above the water, which the paddlers have to pass between

Greco-Roman style of wrestling where only grips above the waist are allowed

heat race in the first round of competition

knockout stage part of a competition where losing means that you are out of the competition for the top prize

MMA short for mixed martial arts, a type of fighting that uses lots of different fighting techniques

modern pentathlon contest made up of four events: fencing, swimming, show jumping, pistol shooting and cross-country running (the last two are combined into one event)

motto words showing the most important beliefs of a person or organisation

open water area for swimming outdoors, such as a river, lake or the sea

pétanque game in which competitors try to throw a heavy ball as close as possible to a small target ball

quarantine rules controlling the animals and other things that can come into a country

relay race in which the athletes race one after the other

USSR Union of Soviet Socialist Republics, a country that existed between 1922 and 1991

Index